BHUTAN

The Land of Dragon People

BHUTAN

The Land of Dragon People

Text & Photographs by
Sneh Shukla

Winsome Books India

ISBN : 81-88043-69-9

First Published 2011

Published by :

Winsome Books India

209, F-17, Harsha Complex, Subhash Chowk,
Laxmi Nagar, Delhi - 110 092
Ph. : 011-65845445
E-mail : winsomebooks@rediffmail.com
admin@winsomebooks.com
Website : www.winsomebooks.com

BHUTAN FACTS

Capital	:	Thimphu.
Currency	:	Ngultrum (BTN).
Government	:	Constitutional Monarchy; special treaty relationship with India.
Cities	:	Thimphu - The capital city , Jakar - An administrative town in the north and the birthplace of Buddhism in Bhutan.,Mongar - One of the largest towns in east Bhutan.,Paro - The location of the international airport and Taktsang Monastery, Punakha - A former winter capital of Bhutan. Still hosts the Monastic Body in Winter, Phuentsholing - A town on the Indian border. The point of entry for travelers arriving by bus from Kolkata. Samdrup Jongkhar - An administrative town in the southeast, near the Indian border.,Trashigang - A picturesque administrative town in the east, Trongsa - A small administrative town famous for its dzong and the Tower of Trongsa.

LANGUAGES

Dzongkha (official), Tibetan dialects (among Bhotes), Nepalese dialects (among Nepalese)

ETHNICITY / RACE

Bhote 50%, ethnic Nepalese 35%, indigenous or migrant tribes 15%.

NATIONAL HOLIDAY

January 2 (not fixed) - Winter Solstice (Western Bhutan only)

January 16 (not fixed) - Traditional Day of Offerings (a day to offer food to hungry creatures - celebrated as new year in Eastern Bhutan).

February 21-23 (every year) - Birth Anniversary of HM the Fifth King Jigme Khesar Namgyal Wangchuck .

February 14-15 (not fixed) - New Year (*losar*).

May 2 (every year) - Birth Anniversary of Third king Jigme Dorji Wangchuck .

May 4 (not fixed) - Shabdrung Kuchoe (commemorates the passing of Shabdrung Ngawang Namgyal in 1651 CE).

May 27 (not fixed) - Commemoration of Lord Buddha's Parnirvana.

June 21 (not fixed) - Anniversary of the Birth of Guru Rinpoche.

July 15 (not fixed) - The first sermon of Lord Buddha.

September 13 (not fixed) - Thimphu Drubchen (Thimphu Only).

September 17-19 (not fixed) - Thimphu Tshechu (Thimphu Only).

October 17 (not fixed) - Hindu ceremony of *Dashain.*

October 29 (not fixed) - Descending Day of Lord Buddha.

November 11 (every year) - Birth Anniversary of HM the fourth King Jigme Singye Wangchuck.

December 17 (every year) - National day, commemorating the 1907 coronation of the first hereditary king of Bhutan, Ugyen Wangchuck.

In addition to the above national holidays, there are also Tshechu holidays which are celebrated regionally.

RELIGIONS

Lamaistic Buddhist 75%, Indian and Nepalese influenced Hinduism 25%.

LITERACY RATE

47% (2003 est.).

ECONOMIC SUMMARY

GDP/PPP (2009 est.): $3.763 billion; per capita $5,400. **Real growth rate:** 5%. **Inflation:** 8% **Unemployment:** 4% (2009 est.) **Arable land:** 3%. **Agriculture:** rice, corn, root crops, citrus, foodgrains; dairy products, eggs. **Labor force:** n.a.; note: major shortage of skilled labor; agriculture 93%, industry and commerce 2%, services 5%. **Industries:** cement, wood products, processed fruits, alcoholic beverages, calcium carbide. **Natural resources:** timber, hydropower, gypsum, calcium carbide. **Exports:** $513 million f.o.b. (2008 est.): electricity (to India), cardamom, gypsum, timber, handicrafts, cement, fruit, precious stones, spices. **Imports:** $533 million (2008 est.): fuel and lubricants, grain, machinery and parts, vehicles, fabrics, rice. **Major trading partners:** India, Bangladesh, Japan, Germany, Austria (2004).

COMMUNICATIONS

Telephones : main lines in use: 25,200 (2003); mobile cellular: 22,000 (2005).
Radio broadcast stations : AM 0, FM 1, shortwave 1 (2004).
Television broadcast stations : 1 (2005). **Internet hosts:** 985 (2003).
Internet users : 15,000 (2003).

TRANSPORTATION

Railways : 0 km.
Highways : total : 4,007 km; paved: 24 km; unpaved: 3,983 km (2002).
Ports and harbors : none.
Airports: 2 (2004 est.).

INTERNATIONAL DISPUTES

Approximately 104,000 Bhutanese refugees live in Nepal, 90% of whom reside in seven UN Office of the High Commissioner for Refugees camps; Bhutan cooperates with India to expel Indian separatists.

NATIONAL PARKS

- Jigme Dorji National Park.
- Jigme Singye Wangchuck National Park.
- Royal Manas National Park.
- Thrumshingla National Park.

WILDLIFE SANCTUARIES / NATURE RESERVES

- Bomdeling Wildlife Sanctuary.
- Khaling Wildlife Sanctuary.
- Phibsoo Wildlife Sanctuary.
- Sakteng Wildlife Sanctuary.
- Toorsa Strict Nature Reserve.

SACRED SITES

• Kurje Lhakhang, Jakar. A temple built around a cave with a body print of Guru Rinpoche embedded in the wall. Guru Rinpoche practiced meditation here on his first visit to Bhutan and as such it is the earliest Buddhist relic in the country.

• Taktsang Monastery (Tiger's Nest), Paro. This is one of the most important Buddhist sites in the world, and Guru Rinpoche visited here on his second visit to Bhutan. The temple is built on a 1,200 meter cliff and is Bhutan's most well known sacred site.

• Singye Dzong , Lhuentse. This is is a sacred valley located near the Tibetan border. The main temple in the valley was founded by Yeshi Tsogyal, and Guru Rinpoche visited the region on his second visit to Bhutan. However, partly due to the fact that the valley is in a sensitive area near the border and also partly due to Bhutan wishing to preserve the sanctity of its sacred sites, the valley is not open for tourists.

WHAT TO LEARN IN BHUTAN

Buddhism - It is possible to receive instruction on Buddhist practice at any monastery, though for discussions on Buddhist philosophy it is better to consult with the khenpos or loppons (teachers) at Buddhist colleges (shedra), such as, for example, Lhodrak Kharchhu Monastery in Jakar, Tango Monastery near Thimphu or Chokyi Gyatso Institute in Deothang.

Deer Park Thimphu holds various Dharma related events in the capital, including weekly meditation sessions.

Weaving - Bhutanese woven cloth is prized throughout the world for its unique designs and high quality, and there is a weaving center in Khaling in Trashigang.

CODE OF CONDUCT FOR THE TRAVELLERS

The **king and former king** are accorded a great deal of respect in Bhutan. It is wise to bear this in mind when conversing with local people.

Sacred objects. Always pass mani stones, stupas and other religious objects with your right side nearest to the object, and turn prayer wheels in a clockwise direction. Never sit on mani stones or stupas.

Clothing. When visiting temples, remove shoes and head gear and wear clothing that expresses respect for the sacred nature of the site. You will need to wear pants and long shirts.

Donations. At monasteries, it is custom to make a small donation to the monks as a sign of respect; and also to the Buddhist statues as a means of developing a generous and spacious mind. There are many places in each temple where you can donate, and it is expected that you donate to each place. Remember to have small notes for this gesture. However, this is not mandatory.

Smoking. It is illegal to smoke at monasteries and in public places.

Tobacco. Products containing tobacco (cigarettes, chewing tobacco etc) should not be taken to sacred sites.

BHUTANIES EMBASSIES AND CONSULATES

India : Royal Bhutanese Embassy - Chandragupta Marg, Chanakyapuri, New Delhi 110 021. Tel: 609217/ 609218, Fax:6876710.

U.S. : Consulate General of Bhutan - 2 UN Plaza, 27th Floor, New York NY 10017. Tel:(212) 826-1919, Fax:(212) 826-2998.

Canada : Honorary Consul of Bhutan - 150 Isabella Street, Ottawa, Ontario K1S 1V7. Tel:(613) 232-1222 Fax:(613)569-4667.

Hong Kong : Honorary Consul of Bhutan - 32/F, New World Tower, 16-18 Queen's Road, Central, HongKong, China. Tel : (852) 28443117, 2844-3111, Fax: (852) 25247652 Email: joycecheung@nwd.com.hk

Thailand : The Royal Bhutanese Embassy in Bangkok - Jewelry Trade Center Building, Rm. 1907, 19th Floor, 919/1 Silom Road, Bangkok 10500. Tel:2671722, 630119 - Fax:6301193.

WELCOME TO THIMPHU CITY

BRIEF HISTORY OF BHUTAN

Although archaeological exploration of Bhutan has been limited, evidence of civilization in the region dates back to at least 2000 B.C. Aboriginal Bhutanese, known as Monpa, are believed to have migrated from Tibet. The traditional name of the country since the 17th century has been Drukyul, Land of the Drokpa (Dragon People), a reference to the dominant branch of Tibetan Buddhism that is still practiced in the Himalayan kingdom.

Until the early 17th century, Bhutan existed as a patchwork of minor warring fiefdoms, when the area was unified by the Tibetan lama and military leader Shabdrung Ngawang Namgyal who fled religious persecution in Tibet. To defend the country against intermittent Tibetan forays, Namgyal built a network of impregnable dzong (fortresses), and promulgated a code of law that helped to bring local lords under centralised control. Many such dzong still exist and are active centers of religion and district administration. After Namgyal's death in 1651, Bhutan fell into civil war. Taking advantage of the chaos, the Tibetans attacked Bhutan in 1710, and again in 1730 with the help of the Mongols. Both assaults were successfully thwarted, and an armistice was signed in 1759. In the 18th century, the Bhutanese invaded and occupied the kingdom of Cooch Behar to the south. In 1772, Cooch Behar appealed to the British East India Company which assisted them in ousting the Bhutanese, and later in attacking Bhutan itself in 1774.

A peace treaty was signed in which Bhutan agreed to retreat to its pre-1730 borders. However, the peace was tenuous, and border skirmishes with the British were to continue for the next 100 years. The skirmishes eventually led to the Duar War (1864-1865), a confrontation for control of the Bengal Duars. After Bhutan lost the war, the Treaty of Sinchula was signed between British India and Bhutan. As part of the war reparations, the Duars were ceded to the United Kingdom in exchange for a rent of Rs. 50,000. The treaty ended all hostilities between British

India and Bhutan.

During the 1870s, power struggles between the rival valleys of Paro and Tongsa led to civil war in Bhutan, eventually leading to the ascendancy of Ugyen Wangchuck, the ponlop (governor) of Tongsa. From his power base in central Bhutan, Ugyen Wangchuck defeated his political enemies and united the country following several civil wars and rebellions in the period 1882-1885.

For centuries, Bhutan was made up of feuding regions until it was unified under King Ugyen Wangchuck in 1907. The British exerted some control over Bhutan's affairs, but never colonized it. Until the 1960s, Bhutan was largely isolated from the rest of the world, and its people carried on a tranquil, traditional way of life, farming and trading, which had remained intact for centuries. After China invaded Tibet, however, Bhutan strengthened its ties and contact with India in an effort to avoid Tibet's fate. New roads and other connections to India began to end its isolation. In the 1960s, Bhutan also undertook social modernization, abolishing slavery and the caste system, emancipating women, and enacting land reform. In 1985, Bhutan made its first diplomatic links with non-Asian countries.

A pro-democracy campaign emerged in 1991, which the government claimed was composed largely of Nepali immigrants. As a result, some 100,000 Nepali civil servants were either evicted or encouraged to emigrate. Most of them crossed the border back into Nepal, where they were housed in UN-administered refugee camps. They continue to languish there a decade later.

In 1998, King Jigme Singye Wangchuck, who is Bhutan's fourth hereditary ruler, voluntarily curtailed his absolute monarchy, and in March 2005 released a draft constitution (not yet put to a referendum) that outlined plans for the country to shift to a two-party democracy. In Dec. 2006, he abdicated in favor of his son, and Crown Prince Jigme

Khesar Namgyal Wangchukin became king. Prime Minister Lyonpo Khandu Wangchuk resigned in July 2007 so he could join a political party in anticipation of the country's first elections, scheduled to be held in early 2008. Lyonpo Kinzang Dorji took over as the interim prime minister.

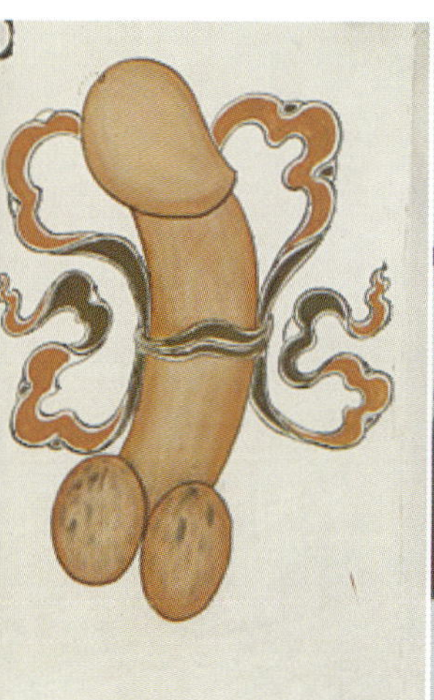

© Reuters

BHUTAN THE ORIGIN OF ITS NAME

Since ancient times Bhutan has been known as a land of mystery. It has been called as Loho mon (the land of darkness) Lho Tsendenjong (southern land of cypress) Lhomen (southern land of four approaches) and Lhojong Menjong (southern land of medicinal herbs), it is in south there before each name southern is added. Only after 17th century its popular name Drkul or land of dragon became popular perhaps it got this from the Buddhist school Drukpa of Vajrayana. According scholars its modern name derived from Sanskrit 'Bhu-uttan' thus Bhutan.

BHUTAN HUNDRED YEARS OF MONARCHY

The history of the Kingdom of Bhutan dates back to 2nd century AD or even further. However, the recorded history is available only from the 7th century AD with the construction of Kyichu lhakhang in Paro and Jampel lhakhang in Bumthang. This was followed by the visit of the Indian saint Guru Rinpoche in the mid-8th century to Bumthang as well as by Lhasey Tsangma, the Tibetan Prince who was exiled from Tibet to Bhutan in the 9th century. He was instrumental in establishing many noble families especially in Eastern and Central Bhutan. The next prominent figure was the visit of Lam Phajo Drugom Zhigpo from Druk Ralung, Tibet in the 13th century considered the forerunner of Drukpa Kagyu school of Buddhism in Bhutan. A wave of many other Lamas from different schools of Buddhism also contributed to the socio-political and religious growth of Bhutan though their visits were marked by constant feuds and schisms.

RKPO
GENERAL, BAR AND RESTAURANT

INTRODUCTION
A fleeting look at the history of pre 1907 Bhutan

The arrival of Zhabdrung Ngawang Namgyal in 1616 brought about a total transformation of the country. Bhutan was unified into one state and a system of governance introduced known as Choesi Nyeden which became a mechanism towards her evolution later as a nation-state. For the first time laws were codified, tax reforms initiated and Dzongs which served as seats of governance built in each region that came under the Drukpa rule.

The next phase of the Bhutanese history is the era of the Desis from 1651 to 1907. Bhutan saw as many as 54 Desis of different competence beginning with Umze Tenzin Drugyal. Intrigues, feuds and clashes between power houses as well as with British-India in the south were a common feature of this era. During this era Bhutan saw as many as six missions and had several clashes with the British-India which ultimately led to the signing of the Treaty of 1774.

The best example of the Bhutanese unity can be seen during the detrimental Ashley Eden mission of 1864 and the ensuing Duar War. Led by Jigme Namgyal, who was then serving as the Trongsa Penlop, the Duar War finally led to the signing of the Treaty of Sinchula in 1865.

This era can be rightfully called the age of Jigme Namgyal as he was the most influential man in Bhutan. As the 48th Druk Desi, he curbed many internal feuds and even after his resignation from the post of Desi in 1873, he remained the main locus of power and an advisor to the central government.

While being able to carve a political niche for himself and emerge as the most powerful personality in the country the Bhutan that he bequeathed to his son Ugyen Wangchuck who was then the Paro Penlop was still marred by intrigues and family feuds. The assassination plan conspired by his adopted brothers Thimphu Dzongpon Alo Dorji and Punakha Dzongpon Phuntsho Dorji led to the battle of Changlimithang of 1885 which is often quoted as the last civil war in Bhutan. Ugyen Wangchuck using his diplomatic skills came out victorious and restored peace and order in the life of the Bhutanese people. A man of vision and a seasoned diplomat he successfully restored the prolonged strained relations between British India and Bhutan by accompanying Younghusband to Tibet in 1904 as a negotiator. As a mark of appreciation for his services he was also accorded with the insignia of the Knight Commander of the Indian Empire.

Gongsa Ugyen Wangchuck was an epitome of bravery, diplomacy, compassion, peace, statecraft and wisdom.

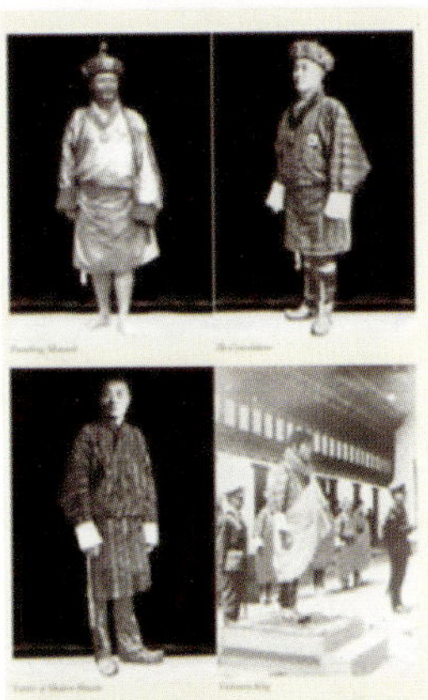

RELIGION

History tells us that in Bhutan Buddhism arrived in sixth century at the same time when it arrived in Tibet. Proper date it unknown but according to King's history when 33rd king Songten Gampo ruled at time Buddhism got it foot hold in Bhutan. King ordered the establishment of monasteries in Himalayan region to subdue the evil spirit. Its growth has been immense and very soon it over powered the local religions. Before Buddhism in Bhutan Bon religion was in practice. Buddhism in Bhutan is by nature Tantrik, it is same like Tibetan Buddhism. It is said that in 7th century Padamsambhava visited Bhutan and laid the foundation of Vajrayana Buddhism.

Buddhism has shapes Bhutanese life and culture, its language art and craft. Its basic social and cultural values are Buddhist. Guru Padamsambhava is patron saint of Bhutan and regarded as second Buddha. After ninth century Buddhism got complete hold on Bhutan and it became major religion of the country. In Bhutan there are hundreds of Buddhist monasteries in which Kyichu Lhakhang of Paro and Lambay Lhakhang of Bhuthang is famous. In Bhutan second most Religion is Hinduism which is practiced in its varied form in various part of Bhutan. Hinduism is Bhutan's oldest religion and exists with Buddhism peacefully.

ESOTERIC BUDDHISM

As above mentioned that in Bhutan major religion is Buddhism but its form is esoteric one that evolved later in Buddhist Mahayana. Esotric Tantrik Buddhism largely follows Toson-kha-pa's version of it described in Snag rm chen mo. According to it Mahayana has two divisions Prajnaparamita and Mantra method and both go together but emphasis is given on mantra method. Esoteric Tantrik Buddhism that beautifully incorporates both parts of Mahayana is known as Vajrayana literally translated as Diamond Vehicle. Vajraya later developed in diverse ways and different then Mahayana in many ways though still considered a branch of it. It s also known as Mantrayana which differs from Parajnaparamita way not only in practice but also in slowness and fastness in attaining the goal of Buddhahood though there is no difference in the conception of Parajnaparamita. Vajrayana though comes into Mahayana but it is a separate path that encapsulates both. In Bhutan according to its way of life an climate it has got a different shade. Overall Bhutanese Buddhism is similar as in Tibet so you may call it Bhutanese Esoteric Buddhism.

PHALLUS

On the walls of Bhutanese houses is commonly seen some painted phallus which used for kind of warding off evils and negative energies. It is a most popular symbol. It comes in different shapes and sizes, carved in wood, metal, stone and cloth. It is painted on walls and hung from the eaves of houses and displayed in various forms during some traditional ceremonies. In Bhutan the phallus is an integral part of ceremonies observed by communities, commonly used to ward off evil spirits and counter evil.

Inauguration of a new house is a sort of phallic ritual whereby the house owner consecrates the house. The ritual is an elaborate one. The ritual constitutes placing of four phalluses on the four eaves of the house facing the four directions and one inside the house. The five giant phalluses carved out from pieces of wood are tied together in a bundle and then put in a bamboo basket. Usually, a young and virgin girl dressed elaborately and leading a dancing and singing troupe carries the basket and circumambulates the house thrice. Then groups of men and women are formed. The women's group stands under the eave of the house facing the east while the male group climbs up on the roof. The basket is tied on the middle of the rope and a tug of war ensues. While men pull the basket roof-ward, the women pretend to pull it to the ground. But the common understanding is that the basket will have to reach the roof at the end so that the phalluses can be hung from the eaves. The pulling begins and continues as typical phallic songs are sung. After every verse of the song the people watching the ritual echo the word laso

The men pretend to lose the battle and the basket is pulled down. At this, the owner of the house serves ara (home brewed spirit) to the men who pretend to be tired. The ara is supposed to energize the men and the 'pulling' battle continues.

Finally when the basket reaches the roof the men place the phalluses on the eaves. These special phalluses also have a dagger (redi) each tied to them which are painted in five different colours.

The five daggers signify the five different manifestations of Lord Jambayang according to Dasho Lam Sanga. "On the east eave is placed a white dagger representing peace, purity, and harmony, a red coloured dagger representing wealth and power is placed on the west, the yellow dagger representing prosperity is placed on the south, and on the north is placed the green dagger representing protection. The fifth dagger placed inside the house is usually blue in colour and symbolizes wisdom." It is sometimes called Kharam shing or Mikha, meaning a piece of wood to counter the evil tongue and eye, Gulang or Wangchu Chenpo, a reference to Lord Shiva, Wangchu Chenpo pho taag, meaning the male symbol of Lord Shiva, or simply Zur shing, meaning a piece of wood that hangs from the eaves. But contrary to the popular perception, the phallus has a world of meaning beyond its obvious symbolism to ward off evil influences. Speaking to Kuensel, a Bhutanese scholar said that the real significance of the phallus has been perverted by popular belief.

BHUTANESE CULTURE AND PEOPLE

Bhutan has a rich and unique cultural heritage that has largely remained intact because of its isolation from the rest of the world until the early 1960s. One of the main attractions for tourists is the country's culture and traditions. Bhutanese tradition is deeply steeped in its Buddhist heritage. Hinduism is the second dominant religion in Bhutan, being most prevalent in the southern regions. Both religions co-exist peacefully and receive support from the government, and enjoy royal patronage. The government is increasingly making efforts to preserve and sustain the current culture and traditions of the country. Because of its largely unspoiled natural environment and cultural heritage, Bhutan has been referred to as *The Last Shangri-la*.

The National Dress for Bhutanese men is the *gho*, a knee-length robe tied at the waist by a cloth belt known as the *kera*. Women wear an ankle-

length dress, the *kira*, which is clipped at one shoulder and tied at the waist. An accompaniment to the kira is a long-sleeved blouse, the *toego*, which is worn underneath the outer layer. Social status and class determine the texture, colours, and decorations that embellish the garments. Differently coloured scarves and shawls are important indicators of social standing, as Bhutan has traditionally been a feudal society. Jewellery is mostly worn by women, especially during religious festivals and public gatherings. To strengthen Bhutan's identity as an independent country, Bhutanese law requires all Bhutanese citizens to wear the national dress in public areas and as formal wear.

Rice, buckwheat, and increasingly maize, are the staple foods of the country. The local diet also includes pork, beef, yak meat, chicken, and mutton. Soups and stews of meat and dried vegetables spiced with chillies and cheese are prepared. *Ema datshi,* made very spicy with

cheese and chilies, might be called the national dish for its ubiquity and the pride that Bhutanese have for it. Dairy foods, particularly butter and cheese from yaks and cows, are also popular, and indeed almost all milk is turned to butter and cheese. Popular beverages include butter tea, tea, locally brewed rice wine and beer. Bhutan is the only country in the world to have banned the sale of tobacco.

Bhutan's national sport is archery, and competitions are held regularly in most villages. It differs from Olympic standards in technical details such as the placement of the targets and atmosphere. There are two targets placed over 100 meters apart and teams shoot from one end of the field to the other. Each member of the team shoots two arrows per round. Traditional Bhutanese archery is a social event and competitions are organized between villages, towns, and amateur teams. There are usually plenty of food and drink complete with singing and dancing. Attempts to distract an opponent include standing around the target and making fun of the shooter's ability. Darts (*khuru*) is an equally popular outdoor team sport, in which heavy wooden darts pointed with a 10 cm nail are thrown at a paperback-sized target ten to 20 meters away.

Another traditional sport is the *digor*, which resembles the shot put and horseshoe throwing. Cricket has gained popularity in Bhutan, particularly since the introduction of television channels from India. The Bhutan national cricket team is one of the more successful affiliate nations in the region. Football is also an increasingly popular sport.

ART AND CRAFT

Bhutan's culture is intact and this lack has been beneficial for the kingdom, its economic and social life evolved independently and creatively. Bhutanese culture is imaginative, practice of Buddhism provides it with all intellectual and cultural material with which people grew in various directions. Strong foundation of Buddhism and its ethics provided people with strong moral and ethical life. Humanism is practiced widely, people are compassionate and loving. But with time Bhutan is destined to change; now monks transcribe ancient Buddhist texts into laptop computers, traditionally-dressed archers use alloy steel bows and arrows, and video rental shops, television, internet has opened them to the new world. Bhutan has been described as 'a living museum' because its ancient dzongs and temples are still the focus of modern life, which is still true.

Amidst so many changes something is eternal which remains intact. Every aspect of life in the kingdom is guided by the ethics of its official religion, Drukpa Kagyu Buddhism. All Bhutanese art, dance, drama and music are steeped in Buddhism: paintings are not produced for tourists, but for religious purposes; festivals are not quaint revivals, but living manifestations of a national faith; and almost all art, music and dance represent the struggle between good and evil. These traditions can be seen in all their glory at Bhutan's spectacular religious festivals called tsechus.

In art it has a rich tradition that no doubt comes from Buddhism. From Thanka to Idol making it follows the ancient Buddhist principle of art. In Thanas they narrate religious beliefs and social and moral values. In its esoterism Bhutanese art equates with Tibetan sacred art. Bhutanese art is strict and follow strict rule of Buddhist iconography, this itself is considered a kind of sadhana. It is believed that by creating this sacred art one earns merit and receives Buddha's blessings. In Bhutan the series of traditional skills or crafts is defined as zorig chusum (zo = the ability

to make; rig = science or craft; chusum = thirteen). The Great Treasure Discoverer, Pema Lingpa introduced the art taught in Bhutan today, in the fifteenth century. In 1680 Shabdrung Nagawang Namgyel ordered the establishment of the school for instruction in the 13 traditional crafts. Although the skills existed well before, across the country's isolated settlements, it is believed that the zorig chusum was first formally categorised during the rule of Tenzin Rabgye (1680-1694), Bhutan is well known for Zorig Chusum which include everything from shingzo i.e. wooden work to clay work and bronze casting, painting, leather work, weaving, black smithy and gold and silver smithy, tailoring. Bhutanese artist's skill is one of the best in the world that can be seen in temple deities, door crafts, thanka, wooden crafts and various architectures.

ARCHITECTURE

Bhutan Architecture is different of its In terms of quality and originality, Bhutanese architecture is without doubt one of the best expressions of the Thunder Dragon Kingdom's unique character. Almost completely isolated for many centuries by its complex geography, Bhutan has indeed seen very few changes in its architecture. Bhutanese architecture is known as **Dzong architecture** is fortress architecture found in the former and present Buddhist kingdoms of the Himalayas, most notably Bhutan. The architecture is massive in style with towering exterior walls surrounding a complex of courtyards, temples, administrative offices, and monks' accommodation.

Some of its features include :1- High inward sloping walls of brick and stone painted white with few or no windows in the lower sections of the wall 2 - Use of a surrounding red ochre stripe near the top of the walls, sometimes punctuated by large gold circles. 3 - Use of Chinese-style flared roofs atop interior temples. 4 - Massive entry doors made of wood and iron5- Interior courtyards and temples brightly colored in Buddhist-themed art motifs such as the ashtamangala or swastika. Dzongs serves as the religious, military, administrative, and social centers. Its traditional Buddhist architecture so it is constructed under the direction of a high Lama who establishes each aspect and dimension by means of spiritual inspiration. With time though Bhutan is changing and modern style architecture is now taking place.

BHUTANESE FOOD

Almost all Bhutanese meals consist of a generous helping of rice and one or more "curry" dishes. In Dzongkha those dishes are called ***tshoem.*** The rice is boiled (or steamed) and can be white polished rice (called ***ja chum***)or a unique variety of Bhutanese rice which is pink in color (called ***eue chum***). The pink or red sice is heavier and has a slightly nutty flavour. The basic principle behind most Bhutanese dishes is pretty simple... "Water, butter, boil!" (I'm stealing this quote from a friend). Most of the dishes are boiled in water with some oil and other garnishing. The method is so simple yet you can get a lot of dishes done this way. (A word of caution, most beginners in Bhutanese cooking tend to flood their dishes, use small amounts of water and add more as you go). The real differences come from the main ingredients. These can be common stuff like beans or potatoes to exotic delicacies like orchids, fern fronds and canes. These can be dried or fresh, depending on the season.

One of the most distinguishing features of Bhutanese is the ubiquitous chilli. People like their food hot, and the chilli can be fresh green ones, dried red chillies or chilli powder. That may also not be enough - raw chillies can be eaten dipped in salt to accompany a dish or ***esay*** can accompany a meal. The ***esay*** serves a similar function as the pickle in Indian cooking and resembles the Mexican salsa. Cheese is another favourite ingredient and infact ***era datshi***is one of the most popular dishes in Bhutan. This is a super hot dish comprising mainly of chilli and cheese.

Some popular vegetarian dishes : **Ema-datsi.** Ema (Chili) and datsi (a kind of cottage cheese) a hot favorite for the young and old. A rare combination of cheese an chilies which is a featured menu in every household.

Kewa-datsi. Kewa (potato) datsi (cheese) a yummy potatoey cheesy dish.

Shamu-datsi. Shamu (mushroom) datsi (cheese) a truly rich and delicious dish. Kewa-datsi and shamu-datsi are less spiced up and go well with red rice.

Cheese momo. Are dumplings filled with cheese and veggies like cabbage, spinach and onions. They usually served with ezay (chili chutney).

Khuli. Buckwheat pancakes- goes well with ema-datsi

Non-vagiterian Dishes : Kewa Phagsha - (Spicy Pork with Potatoes), Jasha Maroo (Minced Chicken), Kangchu Maroo (Trotter Tshoem)

FESTIVALS

In addition to the standard Buddhist festivals, there are yearly festivals celebrated with great fanfare in each district. The most renowned of these are the Tsechu (10th day) festivals, commemorating Padmasambhava, locally referred to as 'Guru Rimpoche' this eighth century master, introduced the Nyingma school of Buddhism in Bhutan. Most festivals lasts from three to five days - one of which, usually, falls on the 10th day of the lunar calendar.

The regional Dzong and remote village communities hold their distinct annual Tsechu festival, providing the local populace with a wonderful occasion to dress up, gather together, and enjoy, in a convivial light-hearted atmosphere. It is also an occasion to renew their faith and receive blessings by watching the sacred dances, or receiving 'empowerment' from a lama or Buddhist monk.

The dances, each aspect of which has a symbolic meaning, are performed by trained monks and laymen wearing ornate costumes, and, in some cases, impressive masks. At Paro, Wangdu, Mongar and Tashigang, among other places, a large 'thanka' scroll known as a Tongdrol is exhihited for a few hours, at day break of the final day of the festival, enabling the people to obtain its blessing, since such scrolls confer liberation by the mere sight of it.

NATURE AND WILDLIFE

Bhutan is no ordinary country. What to make of a country where buying cigarettes is illegal, the rice is red, and where chillies aren't just a seasoning but the entire dish. What to make of a country where archery is their national sport and the one main road has an average of 17 curves per kilometer (no wonder it takes 3 days to go about 150 miles)! Where else on the planet do most men and women still wear their national dress? Only in Bhutan did the king recently push the country to a democracy. And where else in a country about the size of Switzerland does the elevation change from 23,000 feet to 300 feet in not so many miles?

Located in the heart of the high Himalayan mountain range, Bhutan is completely landlocked and is surrounded by mountains in the north and west, by the very rugged terrain of the little known Indian state of Arunachal Pradesh to the east, and by the plains and jungles of Northeast India on the south. Some of the highest mountains in the world separate Bhutan from Tibet to the north.

The population of about 700,000 is made up primarily of indigenous Bhutanese. In the higher reaches of the kingdom and in some isolated valleys live many nomadic tribes that bear a close affinity to similar tribes across the border. Some, like those from Merak and Sakten in the east and Laya in the north, have almost no contact with western civilization and trade only in bartered goods.

29 05 2008 07:28

Royal Bhutan Airlines
Drukair

Royal Bhutan Airlines
Drukair